TH PENTECOST

BY
ZOLA LEVITT

This book is dedicated in the memory of:

Frank John Mack, Jr.
Jerusalem
Feast of Tabernacles, 5745

ZOLA LEVITT

Zola Levitt is a Jewish believer thoroughly educated in the synagogues and brought to the Messiah in 1971. He holds degrees from Duquesne University, Indiana University and an honorary Th.D. from Faith Bible College. He has, in his Christian walk, addressed millions of people concerning the facts of the Bible through his national television program, **ZOLA LEVITT PRESENTS,** which is carried on the major Christian networks, CBN, PTL, TBN and LBN, and numerous large city broadcast stations.

Zola Levitt Ministries, Inc. is a teaching and evangelistic association guided by the standard of Rom. 1:16, "To the Jew first, and also to the Gentile." Like the apostle Paul, we work through the Gentiles to reach the Jews. We inform our Gentile viewers and listeners of those principles of the faith which will be most helpful to them in understanding and witnessing to their Jewish friends. Our ministry offers a wide variety of teaching materials including books, cassette tapes, music, video tapes, and some imported gift items from the Holy Land. A current list of these materials is available at no charge by writing to: ZOLA, Box 12268, Dallas, TX 75225.

ISBN 1-930749-16-3

I
THE MIRACLE

It was the night of Passover. The disciples were very nervous.

Who could blame them? Their leader, the remarkable Carpenter of Galilee who claimed He was the Son of God, had created quite a stir in Jerusalem the previous Sunday. He had ridden a donkey down the road from Lazarus' home at Bethany, where they had spent the Sabbath, right to the Temple. The people had lined the roadside shouting "Hosanna, blessed is the King of Israel that cometh in the name of the Lord!"

That should have been a joyous occasion indeed, but there were elements observing that crowd who really scared the disciples. These were Pharisees who did not in any way believe that the promised King of Israel had come, or that He was their leader, Jesus of Nazareth. In fact, they were furious at this action of Jesus.

The disciples had come to "expect the unexpected" from the miracle-working Jesus Christ, but this time they felt a great sense of apprehension. Had their leader overstepped Himself? Had He gone too far? The rumors of assassination had been in the air for some time now, and this action — this coming as the King — was bound to aggravate the situation.

They huddled together in the upper room of the home of a friend of Jesus. He had sent them there when they had asked Him where He wanted to celebrate the Passover meal. It was a safe place, but in the midst of hostile Jerusalem how could they feel safe?

Jesus did an amazing thing in that Upper Room. He sent Judas out to do some business of His own, a rather peculiar

thing in view of the circumstances, and then He had washed
the feet of the disciples. He spoke to them profoundly of the
fact that His mission was done and that He was leaving. It
didn't make them feel any better.

He told them, "I go to prepare a place for you." He said,
"In My Father's house are many mansions . . . I will come
again and receive you unto Myself." It was comforting, in a
way, because they all well knew that Jesus' most abstract
predictions had a way of coming out. But these new pro-
nouncements of such gravity had the disciples very concern-
ed. If He were going to leave, who would take care of them?
It had been *His* brilliance, *His* marvelous works, *His* healing,
His teachings, that had sustained them. How would they fare
against the Pharisees and the rest of a misunderstanding people if He left them leaderless? Who could possibly take *His*
place? Who would be there to show them the right way —
the right meaning of God's will? Who but Jesus, with His inspiring life of personal prayer, sinlessness and humility, could
possibly guide them at such a time?

Philip could not hold his peace any longer. He spoke up
and requested of the Lord that He show them the Father! After
all, if He were going to His Father's house, then He could
possibly give them a vision of His Father and they would be
greatly comforted.

But Jesus told Philip, "Have I been so long a time with you,
and yet hast thou not known Me, Philip? He that hath seen
Me hath seen the Father!"

It was an answer typical of Jesus — filled with meaning and
spiritual grace. They had certainly heard Him say enough times
that He was virtually the Father on earth, or at least the Son
of the Father. But again, who would take care of them after
He left?

Jesus went on, "And I will pray to the Father, and He shall
give you another Comforter, that He may abide with you
forever; even the Spirit of truth . . ."

Now that was more like it. Jesus was going to send them
another leader. That He was going to return for them

personally on some future day in order to take them to His
Father's house was good news; but this latter statement —
that He would actually provide them a leader until His coming — well, that was what they wanted to hear!

Jesus went on to describe this "Comforter" He was going
to send: "But the Comforter, which is the Holy Spirit, whom
the Father will send in My name, He shall teach you all things,
and bring all things to your remembrance, whatsoever I have
said unto you." And He concluded, "Peace I leave with
you . . . let not your heart be troubled, neither let it be afraid."

The message was satisfying beyond measure to the disciples.
They eagerly sought this Comforter — this Holy Spirit the Lord
was going to send. They had no idea that night of just *how*
Jesus was going to take His leave, or how the Comforter would
arrive, but they knew Jesus well enough to trust his pro-
nouncements to the letter. The Lord would leave, and the
Spirit would come. They had no reason to be troubled. Hadn't
the Lord Himself said, "Let not your hearts be troubled?"

Jesus taught them in great detail that night, giving them the
feeling that this was the final lesson and that His going was
imminent. He seemed to be instructing them in the fine points
of life without the Savior's presence, and they listened carefully.
Peter particularly, as was his habit, hung on the Lord's every
word.

Eventually they finished the Passover ceremony and retired
to the Mount of Olives where the Lord liked to pass the night
in His own prayers. It was a routine they had observed many
times before in their three years with Him.

But that night turned into one long nightmare!

Judas returned to them, but he brought soldiers! He iden-
tified the Lord for them and they took Jesus into custody. The
disciples were stricken.

Peter stood by as the Lord stood trial, unwilling to admit
that he was one of Jesus' party, and he had to deny this three
times, in fact, before dawn broke. He was miserable about
his denials, but what could he do? They would have killed
him. Peter was never one to oppose the crowd.

The horrible crucifixion took place at nine in the morning as the Romans disposed of Jesus, the King of Israel. They believed He was the king, in their view of "the king", and they wrote as much on His cross. He was certainly not the first nor the last to be crucified by the cruel Roman legions for showing what they thought of as opposition to the state.

The crowd wept. There were many Jewish people who loved Jesus, and many who were His secret followers. To the majority of the crowd who saw the crucifixion, this was their most tragic Passover day.

The Lord's body was interred and a guard placed at the entrance to the tomb. The Romans did not want any body-stealing or posthumous ceremonies following this politically delicate situation.

The disciples went into seclusion, overwhelmed by the monstrosity of the crucifixion of their gentle Lord, and fearful for their own lives in spite of what He had promised. They awaited the Comforter and the Lord's eventual return, and they took courage from these things, but for the moment they were in the dangerous position of subversives at large.

But their fears were only temporary. We can imagine their incredulous elation the following Sunday when they saw that Jesus Christ had defeated death! The tomb was empty; the Savior was gone! He had come back from the dead and the disciples were leaderless no longer!

Jesus joined them soon after and spent the next forty days teaching and encouraging his amazed followers. They were skeptical at first; Thomas wanted some hard evidence that the man who appeared among them now was really Jesus, and he got it! Peter was contrite, of course. Philip was more than satisfied; all his questions were answered. Judas, whose betrayal brought only greater glory to the Lord, had died of suicide on the day of the crucifixion.

Jesus reminded them that the Father was soon to send the Comforter and He counseled them to remain at Jerusalem until that time. The disciples continued their habit of asking many questions about the future — "Lord, wilt thou at this time restore again the kingdom to Israel?" — but the Lord indicated only that once the Holy Spirit would come, "Ye shall receive power . . . and ye shall be witnesses unto Me both in Jerusalem, and in all Judaea, and in Samaria, and unto the uttermost part of the earth."

It was a heartening commission to say the least, and the disciples eagerly awaited the Holy Spirit at Jerusalem. Jesus "was taken up; and a cloud received Him out of their sight." Probably the disciples were not so shaken at this departure of their Lord because the Holy Spirit was surely coming shortly, and because two angels appeared with a faith-building message: ". . . this same Jesus, which is taken up from you into heaven, shall so come in like manner as ye have seen Him go into heaven."

The Lord was going to return for them as He had promised. But first, the Holy Spirit was going to come.

Pentecost, coming in late May or early June, was likely a very beautiful day. It doesn't rain much in Jerusalem and indeed it's hard to find even a stray cloud in the blue sky. The Festival of Weeks, or Pentecost, celebrated the early harvest of the spring, and the major one of the fall to come. It was a joyous occasion which drew the Jewish people from all over Israel and many foreign lands.

Peter and the rest of the disciples were at the Temple bright and early, and possibly they were actually anticipating the appearance of the Holy Spirit that day. After all, they had seen the Lord take action on each of the past three feast days: He was crucified on Passover, buried on Unleavened Bread and resurrected on First Fruits. It is not clear just how much Bible knowledge the tradesmen-disciples had accumulated, but if they were familiar with the order of the Jewish feasts, either as it is given in Leviticus 23, or as they had observed it, they might have had a tingling feeling that Pentecost morning.

The day must have been very still, in terms of breezes, since

Jerusalem is not usually a windy place, and in the summer it is especially peaceful. The huge crowd at the Temple by eight or nine a.m. probably expected nothing unusual.

But ". . . suddenly there came a sound from heaven as of a rushing mighty wind, and it filled all the house where they were sitting!"

That must have been a shock!

And then, ". . . there appeared unto them cloven tongues like as of fire . . . and they were all filled with the Holy Spirit, and began to speak with other tongues, as the Spirit gave them utterance!"

What an incredible moment!

What was happening?

Well, ". . . the multitude came together, and were confounded, because that every man heard them speak in his own language." It seems that the disciples, those ordinary fishermen, tax collectors and work-a-day tradesmen, had suddenly become expert linguists. They were speaking eloquently in the languages of the variety of countries from which the large crowd of worshipers came.

"And they were all amazed and marvelled, saying one to another, Behold, are not all these which speak Galileans?" What they meant by that was simply, *Aren't these fellows from up north in the country? Aren't these men simple folk from the farms and villages of Galilee?"* "And how hear we every man in our own tongue, wherein we were born?"

The second chapter of the book of Acts goes on to explain how many different countries were represented at Pentecost, and a selection of some 16 nations were presented. Obviously the collected Jewish worshipers had among them the speakers of many foreign languages. But the Galileans were equal to the occasion.

One theory that went through the crowd was that the men were drunk. "And they were all amazed and were in doubt, saying to one another, 'What meaneth this?' Others mocking said, 'These men are full of new wine' " (Acts 2:12,13).

At that point Peter stood up and preached one of the most

fruitful sermons in the entire Bible.

He began by pointing out that the men were hardly drunk, "seeing it is but the third hour of the day (9 a.m.)," and he taught that what they were seeing had been in fact prophesied by Joel. He quoted Joel for the mesmerized crowd, "And it shall come to pass in the last days, saith God, I will pour out of my Spirit upon all flesh . . ." He concluded his quotation with Joel's stirring prophecy, "And it shall come to pass, that whosoever shall call on the name of the Lord shall be saved."

Then he went on to exhort the multitude: "Ye men of Israel, hear these words," and he taught them that Jesus Christ has indeed been the Messiah.

The gathered crowd must have been galvanized by this very controversial statement. After all, it had been just seven weeks before that they had seen Jesus, the Carpenter from Nazareth, crucified, and of course they had wrestled with the alleged story of His resurrection. It must have been a spiritual and political issue of the highest import to the people of Israel, and this Feast of Pentecost marked their first gathering together since those critical days of the spring feasts.

Peter went on to point out that the crowd had certainly failed to recognize Jesus as the Messiah and, in fact, "by wicked hands" had Him slain. We can imagine what a stir this must have raised in the holiday gathering.

Peter then reached for yet another Old Testament passage to drive home his point. He spoke of David's 16th Psalm in which David praised God, "Because thou wilt not leave my soul in hell, neither wilt thou suffer thine Holy One to see corruption." By the term "Holy One" David must have been referring to one who would come and not see death, argued Peter. David could not have been referring to himself for, as Peter went on to say, "David is both dead and buried, and his sepulchre is *with us unto this day.*"

Obviously the Jews, who still visit the tomb of King David in Jerusalem today, well knew that their former sovereign lay buried in his capital city. But none of them present that day could have said with any certainty that Jesus Christ was dead.

His tomb, also in Jerusalem, lay empty.

We can almost imagine Peter gesturing in the direction of King David's tomb and the crowd nodding and murmuring among themselves, "That's true, that's true. . ."

"This Jesus hath God raised up," continued Peter, "whereof we all are witnesses." That was a very strong statement, but Peter apparently had no fear of contradiction from the crowd. Had the body of Jesus Christ been produced after all? Had anyone testified to seeing the corpse? Wasn't the tomb empty to this very day after all? Could anyone in the crowd offer that Jesus had *not* been "raised up"?

We can almost see the crowd leaning forward as Peter concluded his explanation of the miracle at Pentecost: "Therefore being by the right hand of God exalted, and having received of the Father the promise of the Holy Ghost, He (Jesus) hath shed forth *this,* which ye now see and hear" (Acts 2:33).

And Peter reached a stirring conclusion: "Therefore let all the house of Israel know assuredly, that God hath made that same Jesus, whom ye have crucified, both Lord and Christ" (Acts 2:36).

The gathered multitude was stricken. The Scripture goes on, "Now when they heard this, they were pricked in their heart, and said unto Peter and to the rest of the apostles, Men and brethren, what shall we do?"

"What shall we do?" What a marvelous question! What a marvelous reaction to the appeal of an evangelist! How successful a sermon must be preached to have the simple response, "What shall we do?"

Peter seized the moment. "Repent, and be baptized every one of you in the name of Jesus Christ for the remission of sins, and ye shall receive the gift of the Holy Spirit. For the promise is unto you, and to your children, and to all that are afar off, even as many as the Lord our God shall call."

The harvest was stunning. "Then they that gladly received His word were baptized: and the same day there were added unto them about three thousand souls."

Three thousand souls! Three thousand new Christians to

add to the young church of Jerusalem. Three thousand Jewish people brought to the Messiah Jesus Christ. What a harvest! Perhaps a Jewish scholar or two in the crowd could think back to a similarly great day on which Moses returned from the mount with the law of God in his hand. That day had a tragic ending, unfortunately, because the people waiting below could not wait and had made a golden calf. The scholars of the Old Testament could remember that on that day three thousand were slain.

Indeed, "The letter kills, the Spirit gives life."

Many Bible readers consider that the end of the miracle of Pentecost, and indeed it seems to be a full day's harvest. But the Scripture goes on in Acts 2, 3 and 4 to indicate that more souls still came to the Lord and that those who had come on the day of the miracle "continued stedfastly in the apostles' doctrine and fellowship, and in breaking of bread, and in prayers." We see that the harvest went on: "And the Lord added to the Church daily such as should be saved."

Shortly thereafter Peter and John went up together into the Temple and encountered a man who had been born lame and who was carried daily to the gate of the Temple where he could beg alms of the worshipers. When the beggar solicited the two apostles, Peter said, "Silver and gold have I none: but such as I have give I thee: In the name of Jesus Christ of Nazareth rise up and walk."

Peter's healing prayer had a profound effect. "And he leaping up stood, and walked, and entered with them into the Temple, walking, and leaping, and praising God. And all the people saw him walking and praising God: And they knew that it was he which sat for alms at the Beautiful Gate of the Temple: and they were filled with wonder and amazement at that which had happened unto him."

During the ministry of Jesus, crowds had seen the Savior also heal, but the Pharisees seemed ever present to doubt the miracles. In the case of the man born blind in John 9, the

Pharisees indicated that the man who was now saying his sight was restored was actually not the same blind beggar they all knew, and they even had a hearing to determine the identity of the supposedly healed man. The blind beggar testified, "whereas I was blind, now I see." But the Pharisees were not very ready to accept that miracle.

But this particular case, happening at the Temple gate, could not be a case of mistaken identity. Obviously *this* beggar was very well known. The people were probably very used to giving him a coin when they entered on the occasions of the feasts, and he was likely a fixture at the holy Temple. There could be no doubt that the remarkable statement of Peter — "in the name of Jesus Christ of Nazareth rise up and walk" — had healed this lame beggar.

Peter again capitalized on the moment. He faced the crowd and stated: "Ye men of Israel, why marvel ye at this? Or why look ye so earnestly on us, as though by our own power or holiness we had made this man to walk?" Peter, of course, denied responsibility that it was his own hand that had caused the healing of the lame man, but instead taught a profound lesson going back to the covenant made with Abraham and to the prophecy of Moses: "A prophet shall the Lord your God raise up unto you of your brethren, like unto me; him shall ye hear in all things whatsoever he shall say unto you." Peter appealed to his brethren as Jews: "Ye are the children of the prophets, and of the covenant which God made with our fathers . . ."; "Unto you first God, having raised up his Son Jesus, sent him to bless you, in turning away every one of you from his iniquities."

At that point the sermon was interrupted as the priests and the Sadducees and an officer of the Temple apprehended Peter and John, "being grieved that they taught the people, and preached through Jesus the resurrection from the dead." Peter and John were detained until the next day and the crowds dispersed, but again there was a mighty harvest: "Howbeit many of them which heard the word believed; and the number of the men was about five thousand."

Imagine Peter, who on the very night of the crucifixion, shrunk from identifying himself with Jesus Christ, denying his Lord three times over, reaping such harvest. What a spiritual giant this man had become. What an evangelist! What a preacher! His scholarship was unerring, his messages devastating. His appeal to faith was irresistible and his zeal for the Lord Jesus Christ inspiring to thousands. We read nowhere else in the new Testament such mighty numbers of salvations, not even in the ministry of the Lord Himself.

But again, as Peter was always the first to say, it was not he but the Lord who healed, who saved, who wrought miracles. Jesus had sent the rushing, mighty wind, taught Peter; Jesus had caused the disciples to speak in the foreign languages sharing their faith in Christ; it was Jesus who obviously sent the tongues of flame; it was Jesus who had been gloriously resurrected and was now calling men to His Church. It was Jesus who sent the Holy Spirit.

And so that was the miracle at Pentecost. It was a Jewish holiday on which remarkable signs and wonders came before the people. Simple Galileans, rural tradesmen, had addressed their brethren of far-off Rome and Libya and Asia, each in their own tongue; Peter, a common fisherman, had taught the Old Testament to the gathered thousands of faithful Jews. Fire from heaven lit the scene, and the Comforter from heaven, whom the Lord had promised, had come to the Chosen People.

Although apparently all of those who were saved were Jews, the demonstration of the foreign languages and the salvation of the travelers from many lands represented a remarkable prophecy that the Church of Jesus Christ would sweep over the world. Today we take for granted that men of all nations become Christians. We do not often stop to realize that the beginning of this remarkable missionary calling which crosses mountain ranges, mighty oceans, "iron curtains," and whole continents, was begun at the Temple of God in Jerusalem. The Church was to sweep away the Roman Empire; the Church was to pervade Asia, the Middle East, the European continent; the Church was to come to the New World, the Church was to pervade the whole of mankind.

Today missionaries go forth throughout the world from all nations, and they must all learn foreign languages. It is many times a slow and difficult process. The calling out of the Church rests in the hands of men in this age of faith. But we cannot help but be inspired by what mighty works were accomplished in a single day at the miracle at Pentecost.

"REPENT AND BE BAPTIZED"

The preceding material was reprinted from the book, Creation of a Masterpiece, by Torger G. Thompson and the author. It is available at the Biblical Arts Center of Dallas where artist Thompson's one-of-a-kind painting of the miracle of Pentecost is on display. This 124' by 20' masterwork must be seen to be appreciated and all readers are referred to it with sincerest commendations. One glance at this heroic artwork is worth a year's study of Acts 2 in realizing the full impact of this singular miracle.

I wanted to add a postscript to the preceding biblical exposition of Pentecost. It has to do with what may be a most important archaeological discovery made in 1976 at the diggings in Jerusalem. I recently visited the Temple site, as I do on a yearly basis, and checked out the latest work going on near the southern wall of the Temple, still standing imposing on Mount Moriah.

And there I saw three mikva'ot, ritual baths.

A mikva'ot is simply a purification pool where the Jews used to wash themselves before entering the Temple (Ex. 29:4, etc.). It was normally dug out of the soil and paved, and it served for the legal ritual as well as providing for a practical matter — the southern wall had the entrance for the plain folks who came into the Temple hot and dusty from the roads and the fields. The Huldah Gate, just up the stairs from the mikva'ot, was used by the poor — and by Jesus and His disciples. The weary worshipers were greatly refreshed here.

I stood by those three dug-outs, each about ten feet long and three feet wide, with remains of the ancient stairs leading down into each one, and I could picture the Lord and His men washing before they entered the Temple proper through the gate of the common people. The Lord will not use the Huldah Gate when He returns, of course. The East Gate — the Golden Gate — is closed now, as prophecy said it would be, but it will open for the King when He comes.

And I realized something else as I examined the ancient baths, one of which actually had water in it, presumably for the use of the workmen at the site who are presently restoring the stairs. What came to my mind was Acts 2:38, "Repent and *be baptized.*" Peter gave this startling command to his 3,000 new converts there at Soloman's portico in the Temple.

We realize that the 3,000 actually *were* baptized (v. 41), but we wonder where?

It has been quite a problem for students of the New Testament. Where did Peter manage to have 3,000 people baptized without creating quite an incident in Jerusalem? After all, with the whole city buzzing about the recent career of the remarkable Carpenter from Galilee, and with the teaching about His resurrection rapidly becoming a police matter (Acts 4:1-3), how was this massive baptism to be accomplished? Where did they find water?

Jerusalem is no place to go for fresh water. There are no rivers or lakes; not even a stream flows through that mountaintop aridness. King Solomon and King Herod, the Temple builders, had managed marvelous feats of engineering in tapping the underground water sources for circulating water to be utilized in the worship, but otherwise there were only a few miserly pools of fresh water spaced throughout the city.

It has been conjectured that Peter led the new followers of the Messiah to the nearby Pool of Siloam, mentioned in the Gospel, for baptism on that Pentecost Sunday. But Siloam is a small pool, not larger than a modest backyard swimming pool. It is quite doubtful that the 3,000 converged in that small space, particularly under the tense circumstances.

But now, with the discovery of the *mikva'ot* right by the Temple wall beneath Solomon's Portico, we come upon a fascinating new theory. Perhaps Peter simply directed his charges to exit through the Huldah Gate (the exit was toward the western side of the southern wall, the entrance toward the east; they led to one-way ramps, suggesting the enormity of the crowds). They would all have gone back through the washing procedure as though entering the Temple for the first time — but this time they would be covertly washed in the name of Jesus Christ.

Even a crowd of 3,000 would have caused no special notice at the *mikva'ot*. Fully three *million* people entered the Temple on a typical Pentecost in that age; we can imagine the noisy throngs normally assembled at the pools on the morning of the first day of the feast. And the *mikva'ot* were intended for just this purpose — the cleansing of the nation at large, the vast number of farmers, tradesmen, fishermen, students, weary travelers and pilgrims who made up a vast majority of the Chosen People of God. Another 3,000 purifying themselves in the *mikva'ot* that morning would have been virtually unnoticeable.

And so Peter may have well said that the multitude newly added to the faith should cleanse themselves once more that memorable morning, but in honor of the sinless Master who Himself did not omit baptism.

Now again, this idea must be taken as a theory. Certainly no one *knows* exactly what happened that morning in terms of baptism. But other alternatives seem improbable. For the huge number of new believers to have gone all the way to the Jordan River, the largest natural body of fresh water near Jerusalem, doesn't seem likely. The trip is lengthy and arduous and the converts would have missed the remaining week of the feast. And they would have been easily spotted. The laver directly in front of the Temple sanctuary contained a large supply of circulating water, but any attempt at Messianic baptism at that Old Covenant site would have caused an international incident, to say the least.

Perhaps we have literally unearthed, via the archaeology at the Temple site, the answer to a biblical secret. Perhaps we have uncovered the original baptistry of the Church.

"UNTO THE UTTERMOST PART OF THE EARTH"

Most students of the New Testament understand that the Church began at Pentecost, but few fully appreciate the mechanism by which the faith of the 8,000 saved at the feast reached the world. Truly, Christianity was able to overwhelm the Roman Empire, progress throughout Europe and the East and finally become the dominant religion of the New World. The salvation through Jesus Christ is now known over the globe; Christianity in some form or other is understood by nearly every nation today.

How did it happen? How did the new faith achieve world importance?

Originally, the Kingdom of Heaven came to Israel, and Israel only:

> Go not into the way of the Gentiles, and into any city of the Samaritans enter ye not. But go rather to the lost sheep of the house of Israel (Mt. 10:5-6).

Then, later on, in what must have been rather a surprising command to the disciples, the Lord changes His instructions:

> But ye shall receive power, after that the Holy Ghost is come upon you: and ye shall be witnesses unto me both in Jerusalem, and in all Judaea, and in Samaria, and unto the uttermost part of the earth (Acts 1:8).

Uniquely, Jesus seems to alter His original plans, and so He in fact did. These new instructions differ from those He gave in the Gospel. But these were His very last words on earth. Now, the difference, of course, was the fact that not enough of

Israel accepted the Messiah for the Kingdom to reasonably begin. It would have been a very small Kingdom, we gather from the Gospel, with its honest reports of skepticism and disbelief through most of Israel. Simply put, not enough people were saved.

And so, 8,000 Jews were brought to faith in Christ at Pentecost. They hailed from various lands, and thus God ingeniously managed to take the Good News "to the Jew first" (Rom. 1:16) but still to involve foreign nations in the birth of the Church.

But how about the Gentiles?

I heard a radio preacher soberly intone, "The Gentile never had a chance until Pentecost." But he was wrong. The Gentile never had a chance at Pentecost either. Pentecost was, and is, a Jewish holy day, kept in honor of the law of Moses (Lev. 23:15-22), and requiring Temple attendance. Only Jews were permitted to enter the Temple proper, where the Holy Spirit came that magnificent morning (and where the healing and sermon of Acts 3 occurred). The Gentiles could visit the 34-acre Temple quadrangle, and indeed a special court was reserved for such visitors and tourists who might enjoy the spectacle and the sacredness of the central shrine of world Judaism, but no Gentile could actually enter the Temple. Truly, there was no chance for the Gentile at Pentecost.

So how did the Gentile get the Good News?

Well, as we all know from the New Testament, the Jews sent missionaries to the Gentiles and brought them to Christ, one by one. But it didn't start at Pentecost; it actually awaited the conversion of the Roman centurion Cornelius at far-off Caesarea. Some Samaritans (the Samaritans were partly Jewish) had been saved (Acts 8), but no apostle had ever approached a Gentile about the Messiah. Why would they have? The Gentiles weren't waiting for a Messiah, it seems. The Lord's new command notwithstanding, nobody ever dreamed of witnessing to Gentiles.

The dramatic Acts 10 recounts the salvation of a number of Gentiles, including Cornelius, but "they of the circumcision which believed (the Jews) were *astonished*, as many as came with Peter, because that on the Gentiles also was poured out the gift of the Holy Ghost" (vv. 44-45). The Jewish believers had simply never seen a Gentile saved. They were downright astonished, as the Scripture relates.

Peter actually ran into some difficulty with the Church fathers back in Jerusalem when he returned from his mission to the household of Cornelius: "They that were of the circumcision contended with him, saying, thou wentest in to men uncircumcised, and didst eat with them" (Acts 11:3). We can imagine the Jewish churchmen objecting, "How in the world can a Gentile believe in Jesus Christ?"

But Peter clarified his remarkable vision from God, and the unprecedented Acts 11:18 states plainly: "Then hath God also to the Gentiles granted repentance unto life."

Then in a very short time — we can read it a few verses below — a powerful mission was sent to the highly Gentile city of Antioch. Paul and Barnabas accomplished a world-changing result there: "And the disciples were called Christians first at Antioch" (v. 26).

And so it went. The Jewish church of Jerusalem, first established at Pentecost, continued to supply spirit-filled missionaries for the salvation of the Gentile world. The dynamic Paul, the former Rabbi Saul of Tarsus, built those Mediterranean churches whose magnificent struggles with a fledgling faith were to inspire the world. And though he wept, "Brethren, my heart's desire and prayer to God for Israel is, that they might be saved" (Rom. 10:1), he persisted in his calling as God's missionary to the nations — the Gentile's Jew.

I bring it all up because my own heart's desire and prayer to God for Israel is the same as Paul's. I am a Jew, a believer in the Jewish Messiah. I love my people and I want to see them saved.

My people received the Holy Spirit on their feast day, Pentecost. *My people* built the first Christian Church. *My people* traveled journeys of terrible hardship and were martyred in their efforts to take the faith in Jesus Christ to the Gentiles.

Now I pray the favor can be returned.

Each of my books have this same appeal on behalf of my people, the Jews, and my regular readers will recognize it immediately. In fact, some of my regular readers have begun the witness to their Jewish friends and have obtained the blessings from that activity that God promised ("I will bless them who bless thee," He told Abraham in Gen. 12:3). And obviously, many Jewish people have been saved — they come to Christ like everyone else, one by one in child-like faith, responding to the fervent prayers of righteous men.

The real story of Pentecost is the calling out of the world Church — the true Church of Jesus Christ. In a way the radio preacher was right — the Gentile did obtain his chance at Pentecost because people who were willing to witness to the Gentiles were saved that day. The Gentiles have come to the Jewish Messiah — that's the real Miracle of Pentecost.

"TO THE JEW FIRST"

After Pentecost and Cornelius and Antioch, the Apostle Paul, called to the Gentiles, found it necessary to write a pointed reminder about the Jews. The Roman Church apparently was not continuing a witness to the Jews (since relations between Rome and Jerusalem were none too good at best) and Paul stated the following:

> For I am not ashamed of the gospel of Christ: for it is the power of God unto salvation to every one that believeth; to the Jew first; and also to the Greek (Romans 1:16).

Of course the message "to the Jew first" bears repeating today since we seem to be taking the Gospel to the Jew *last*, if at all. Today's Jew is difficult to witness to but probably no more difficult that those Peter confronted. For our purposes here I'd like to review the heart of Peter's message, that marvelous proof text from the prophet Joel. Joel had said some truly revolutionary things for his time and Peter was able to take full advantage of the prophet's forecasting.

Peter and the other disciples had become virtual experts on "the things pertaining to the Kingdom of God" in their studies with the Lord following His resurrection (Acts 1:3). They had thoroughly learned the Old Testament, and therefore Peter was able to rise to the occasion when the opportunity presented itself at Pentecost. We should certainly do no less. In order to witness to the Jew a knowledge of the Old Testament is certainly handy. "The things pertaining to the Kingdom of God" are explained largely in the Old Testament, and for this reason the present day Church is not very aware of them. In de-emphasizing the Old Covenant we also de-emphasize some important passages about our own future.

An examination of the vital five verses of Joel that Peter quoted will provide a very good example. In that short passage we find Joel explaining entirely new concepts of salvation to his astonished audience centuries before Christ:

> And it shall come to pass afterward, that I will pour out my spirit upon all flesh; and your sons and your daughters shall prophesy, your old men shall dream dreams, your young men shall see visions (Joel 2:28).

Here Joel is obviously announcing what we recognize as the coming of the Holy Spirit. But to his Old Covenant listeners it was certainly something new. Prophets prophesied in those olden days, not the mere sons and daughters of the ordinary people. But of course with the advantage of hindsight we have seen the miracles of the Church Age and we have seen our old men "dream dreams" and our young men see visions. Most anyone in the Church can readily think of examples.

Joel went on with another extraordinary statement:

> And also upon the servants and upon the handmaids in those days will I pour out my spirit (vs. 29).

Obviously Joel's listeners had not pictured mere servants and handmaids displaying God's spirit. They were more used to seeing the priests of the Temple, or those with a special calling of God, displaying spiritual gifts. To see King David successfully battle Goliath was to appreciate that the man was anointed of God. But the idea of ordinary people by the multitudes possessing the very spirit of God was something new. One is reminded of Peter's listeners — still very much Old Covenant believers — protesting, "Are not all these which speak Galileans?" (Acts 2:7) What surprised them was that the very plain folks from "the sticks" were speaking the foreign tongues so expertly. They might not have been quite as surprised if educated Pharisees had come forth with that startling miracle.

But it's very evident in the world today that God is choosing "the servants and the handmaids" to take the truth of the Gospel forth. We in the Church are truly Galileans, hopefully as meek as Peter and the others. We do what we do by the enabling ministry of the Holy Spirit.

Joel went on:

> And I will shew wonders in the heavens and in the earth, blood, and fire, and pillars of smoke. The sun shall be turned into darkness, and the moon into blood, before the great and terrible day of the Lord come (vs. 30-31).

Here Joel is referring to the return of the Lord. He describes the fearsome miracles that will take place at the Second Coming and uses the easily identifiable phrase "the great and terrible day of the Lord". Like the other Old Testament prophets, Joel utterly skips over the Church Age, having in view only the coming of the Holy Spirit and then the beginning of the Kingdom of God. The Church Age is, in effect, a problem that arose when Israel failed to receive the Messiah. It's now our problem.

The next verse of Joel, the final one quoted by Peter, has the truly revolutionary message:

And it shall come to pass, that whosoever shall call on the name of the Lord shall be delivered: for in Mount Zion and in Jerusalem shall be deliverance, as the Lord hath said, and in the remnant who the Lord shall call (Joel 2:32).

We should take this three-part verse a part at a time to appreciate its character. First of all, the Old Covenant believers were certainly not convinced that those who would merely "call on the name of the Lord" would be saved. After all, these people were used to making animal sacrifices, keeping a complex law, and trembling before the God of Israel for mere covering of their sins. Many of them had called on the name of the Lord, no doubt, but there was certainly no promise of deliverance in that small act. The entire weight of the law and the sacrificial system rested on each supplicant. But Joel seemed to speak of a time when it would only be necessary to ask for the Lord to deliver one. He seemed to say that anyone who would only call on the name of the Lord would be saved. That must have been shock No. 1 to Joel's listeners.

The second part of the verse was more in keeping with what the Old Covenant believers were accustomed to. Certainly "in Mount Zion and in Jerusalem shall be deliverance as the Lord has said". What Joel seemed to be saying was that prayer and sacrifices, as normally done at the Temple of Jerusalem, would provide deliverance. But deliverance is rather a strong term for what the law actually accomplished. The sacrifices merely covered the sins of Israel; they did not guarantee salvation. Only the Messiah could utterly forgive sins and provide salvation when He came (Romans 3:23-25). God would go along with an unregenerate people as long as their sacrifices were made, but He had not in fact promised the ultimate deliverance except through the Messiah. Here Joel seems to be saying that authentic salvation would be arranged for in Jerusalem someday.

And in Joel's remarkable third statement in this verse, he says plainly that salvation will be available not only in the

Messiah personally but "in the remnant whom the Lord shall call". Could he actually mean that mere men could somehow dispense eternal life? Did he mean to imply that this "remnant" would be followers of the One who would provide salvation in Jerusalem someday?

Indeed he did, we can say with hindsight, since anyone of us who is saved can testify to that precious everlasting life to any other person who will hear it. And this is the force of Joel's message. The Gospels tell us that what we forgive here on earth will be forgiven in heaven. And in point of fact, each born-again believer is a priest, fully able to bring unbelievers before the Lord for salvation. In point of fact, Peter was one of that remnant who the Lord called, and so is every reader of this book who is saved.

And so Peter capitalized on exactly the passage, out of all of those Messianic statements of the Old Testament prophets, which most pointedly explained the miracle at Pentecost. Indeed, the mere handmaids and servants, the remnant, "the Galileans," had the power of the Spirit of God, and the situation remains the same today.

This is a stumbling block for the Jew and for most anybody else as well. The world at large thinks little of the true Church because we are, in fact, mostly handmaids and servants. The more perfect followers we are of Jesus Christ, the more humble and meek we appear to the world. But that in turn — that very humility — is the characteristic of the presence of the Holy Spirit.

We should fully realize that Joel was not merely pointing to Pentecost, but to the entire Church Age up until "the great and the terrible day of the Lord". As that day has not come yet, we are still under the ministry of Pentecost and still going forth from Jerusalem to provide salvation for all who will hear the remnant. We have a most serious responsibility to continue the Pentecostal ministry vested in us today.

Pentecost is the fourth Jewish feast of the festival year as given in Lev. 23. Passover was fulfilled by the crucifixion of the Lord, Unleavened Bread by His burial, and First Fruits by His resurrection. Pentecost, as we have seen, was the harvest. And now we await the fifth feast, Trumpets. When the trumpet sounds, the harvesting is over and we will join the Lord (1 Thes. 4:16-17; 1 Cor. 15:51-52). But until that time, we are still under the orders of Joel and Peter, and the miracle of Pentecost. In effect we have until September each year, since Trumpets occurs then. Pentecost is in June and we are presently making our way through the long summer season of planting and harvest.

The sound of the trumpet will end it all very quickly. Under the old law, when the trumpet sounded the harvest was over and the believers immediately reported to the Temple. Let us keep in mind that there is an ending to what we are doing. We cannot witness forever to our neighbors and friends and family. There will come a day when the trumpet will sound, and salvation will no longer be available from this particular remnant.

And all around, the unbeliever is crying with the prophet Jeremiah,

The harvest is past, the summer is ended, and we are not saved (Jer. 8:20).

STUDY BOOK SERIES by Zola Levitt

THE MIRACLE OF PASSOVER:
A complete explanation of the beautiful symbols and shadows of the Messiah which appear in this crown jewel of Jewish Holy Days. The true meaning of Communion as the Lord instituted it and as the Church practices it.

THE SPIRIT OF PENTECOST:
From the fear and trembling of the Upper Room to the magnificent miracle of the coming of the Holy Spirit. An exciting presentation of the full meaning of "the birthday of the Church."

A CHRISTIAN LOVE STORY:
The Jewish wedding customs of the Messiah's time and how He fulfilled them all in calling out His Bride, the Church. A new and deeper understanding of the bond between the Bridegroom and each believer — a spiritual "Love Story".

THE SIGNS OF THE END:
The Messiah's own words of warning about the conditions that would prevail in the world at the end of God's plan. Are we now approaching the Great Tribulation and the return of our King?

GLORY: The Future of the Believers:
The entire prophetic system explained for those who are going to live it! The Rapture, our time in Heaven, the Kingdom and eternity. Where we go from here. Our rewards, our eternal lives, our entire future.

THE SEVEN FEASTS OF ISRAEL:
A complete explanation of the holy days God gave Moses on Mount Sinai, and how each was fulfilled by our Lord. Passover, Pentecost, Trumpets, Tabernacles, etc., fully discussed as to their hidden meanings in the Messiah. A very special section on how every baby in the womb develops according to God's system of the holy days.

THE SECOND COMING:
The prime difference between the biblical faith and worldly religions is that with the Messiah we have a bright future. What we see is not all we get. The life in this world is of little importance to those who have been promised the Kingdom to come. The return of the King fully explained.

SEVEN CHURCHES: Does Yours Fit In?:
A refreshing and unusual perspective on the churches presented in Revelation 2 and 3. A Jewish Christian and Bible scholar, Zola looks at these earliest churches from the Old Testament and Jewish traditional point of view. A highly interesting and most useful study, applicable to church life everywhere today.

HOW CAN A GENTILE BE SAVED?:
Christians always ask Zola, "How did you come to the Lord?" Their **real** question is, "How can a Jew be saved?" He finally decided to make a biblical inquiry into how **they** got saved. The results are extremely thought-provoking.

"IN MY FATHER'S HOUSE":
The Lord said, "In my Father's house are many mansions . . . I go to prepare a place for you." An explanation of the incredible seven years we will spend as guests in heaven, in the Messiah's Father's house.

ISRAEL, MY PROMISED:
Has God finished with the Jews? Are the modern Israelites the valid Chosen People of the Bible? A sensitive and very personal look at the land of our Lord, as seen today and as promised in the Kingdom.

A current list of Zola Levitt's books, tapes, albums, etc. is available at no charge from:

ZOLA
P.O. Box 12268
Dallas, Texas 75225

Production by:
Great Impressions Printing & Graphics